Selling Your Home Without A Real Estate Agent

Kirk Austin

DEDICATION

This book is dedicated to all the Real Estate agents that put in countless hours helping the members of their communities buy and sell homes.

CONTENTS

1. <u>INTRODUCTION</u>

How To Sell Your Home Yourself, For The Highest Possible Price, And Avoid Paying A Big Commission!

Like thousands of other homeowners, you want to sell your house. Except unlike most homeowners, you want to sell it yourself, without the use of a REALTOR®.

Why? Probably **because you want to save the commission!**

Sure! Why not?! We can't blame you one bit! The thought of saving thousands of dollars certainly is appealing.

We are not like most real estate agents who will try to convince you that selling your home yourself is silly. In fact, if you are willing to learn the process, and invest the time and money to do it, you **can** sell your home yourself, ***and save thousands of dollars in real estate agent's commissions.***

THIS BOOK WILL SHOW YOU HOW, STEP BY STEP!

The techniques and suggestions in this Book are not just some random ideas thrown together. They have been tested and proven over many years and thousands of successful sales.

This Book is organized, and right to the point. Everything you need to know is here, but there's not a lot of fluff thrown in that would waste your time. (You will need every minute to work on the sale!)

Before we get started, we know that you may be thinking:

"Hey, wait a minute! Why in the world would a real estate agent want to show me how to sell my home myself?"

It does seem a little odd, but there is a perfectly logical explanation.

We mentioned before that we are not like most other agents you will meet. We know that what goes around comes around.

We will do everything we can to assist you so that you can achieve your goal of selling your home yourself, and there is absolutely **no obligation!**

Here is the reason why:

The facts are that nearly 90% of all the people who put their home up for sale by themselves eventually end up listing with an agent.

If your situation changes and you decide to list with an agent, we hope that you will allow us to show you our marketing plan and that you will at least consider us for the job.

If you are successful selling your home yourself (and your chances are excellent with the tips in this Book), experience has proven to us that you may remember the help that we provided and give our names to others who might need our services.

In fact, we get just as many referrals from people who were successful selling on their own than the ones who end up listing. So we actually hope that you do achieve your goal and sell it!

No matter what happens, though, it is okay with us. We know that in the long run if we help enough people to get what they want, we will get what we want - which is to make a good living by providing top-notch service to our clients.

So there you have it, pure and simple.

2. GETTING YOUR HOME SOLD

Now let's move on to the real task at hand - *getting your home sold!!!!!*

You **can** sell your home yourself, without listing it with a real estate agent. But there are many things to be done, which means that YOU need to do the work of the agent. If you are willing to put in the effort and learn the process that top agents use, your chances of success will increase greatly.

First off, you need to adopt a business attitude about the entire situation.
Homeowners are often quite emotional about their homes, and it can prevent them from making rational decisions when selling.

They reminisce about all of the holiday get-togethers, backyard barbecues, and how the family grew together in the home.

Please realize that potential buyers are not interested in nor are they affected by your emotional attachments to your home!

They are not looking to buy your home; they are looking to buy a house that they can make into their home.

You must put your emotions aside and realize that you are going to have to make a dollars and cents business transaction.

Studies have shown that home sellers want three main things:

1. To sell their home for the highest possible price.

2. To sell their home within the time frame they need.

3. To sell their home with the least amount of hassle and inconvenience.

If you are like most sellers, you probably want the same things. Only since you are selling it yourself, you are willing to give up some on #3, because you are going to have to take on the work that a real estate agent would normally do.

Yes, that's right!

YOU MUST DO THE JOB OF THE REAL ESTATE AGENT!

It can be a very overwhelming task, so the best way to tackle it is to learn and understand the six-step home selling process:

Step #1 - Understanding Market Conditions and Pricing Your Home

Step #2 - Calculating Your Bottom Line

Step #3 - Preparing Your Home For Sale

Step #4 - Marketing and Showing Your Home

Step #5 - Negotiation and Contract

Step #6 - Closing and Moving

Let's get right to it, and examine the six steps in closer detail!

3. UNDERSTANDING MARKET CONDITIONS

Step #1 - Understanding Market Conditions and Pricing Your Home

This is by far the most important, yet most often misunderstood step. **Failure to understand the market and properly price your home is the single biggest factor that will cause it to NOT SELL for top dollar and sit unsold for months on end!**

To make sure that this does not happen to you, you must first focus on two main areas:

1. CURRENT MARKET CONDITIONS

2. YOUR TIME REQUIREMENTS

Let's look at how current market conditions can effect selling and pricing.

Suppose that there were very few homes on the market for sale, and a large amount of eager buyers. What would that do to prices?

That's right, they would go up. This is referred to as a **seller's market.**

Conversely, if there were very few buyers and lots of eager sellers, what would that do to prices?

Sure, they would go down. That would be a **buyer's market.**

It is the basic law of supply and demand.

Of course, that is a very simple example. The local market may be at one of the extremes, or anywhere in between. You must consider things like interest rates, new home sales, and local economic factors such as zoning changes, large businesses opening or closing, etc.

To properly analyze your current market conditions, you will need to research homes currently available, under contract, and recently sold in your area.

There are several ways to get information on homes that have sold.

The first way is to do the research yourself. The sales prices of homes that have sold and closed is public record, so you can go to your county or city records office and dig for all of the information. I do not know exactly how long it would take, but do not make any other plans that day!

Many title companies will provide you with data on sold homes. Most will do this for free in order to entice you to use them for your title insurance policy.

To get the most complete information, give us a call! With the click of a few buttons on the computer, we can have a complete computerized market analysis of your area - including available, under contract, and closed homes, average price per square foot, and average days on the market, etc. - printed out in a matter of minutes!

We will be happy to bring it over to you, **_with absolutely no obligation, sales pitch, or pressure to list._**

Once you have the market information on homes in your area, take some time and drive around the area, stopping in front of the homes on your list. Make notes about the appearance and other details of the homes.

If any of the available homes are having an open house, take a look inside. Be up front with the owner or agent, and tell them, "We live in the area and are planning to sell our home ourselves. Do you mind if we take a quick look?"

This driving around is an important step, because it gets you more familiar with the market, and will help you make a more objective decision on pricing your home. Next, sit down at the table and review the data and make honest, unbiased comparisons based on criteria such as:

- SIZE
- AGE
- BEDROOMS
- BATHROOMS
- POOL or SPA
- LANDSCAPING
- GARAGE
- VIEW
- LOT SIZE
- OTHER FEATURES AND UPGRADES

Start by taking a brief look at the homes that are currently available for sale. The purpose of looking at the "available" is to get a feel for what other people in your area are asking, NOT to use the information to base your price.

A seller can ask any price for their home, regardless of what it is really worth. Many of the available homes are priced in "dreamland". These prices DO NOT reflect the realities of the market.

In fact, professional appraisers cannot use available prices at all when appraising a house, only closed sales within the past six months!

Now move on to the pending and closed sales. **This is the real bottom line, where the "rubber meets the road". It is the hard reality - what buyers were willing to pay and what sellers were willing to sell for in a free, open market.**

Study the closed sales. The first thing you may discover is that the actual sales price of the neighbor's home that sold 2 months ago is less than what they told you when you saw them out in the driveway. *Imagine that!*

Identify the homes that are similar to yours, ones that are nearly the same size, style, etc. Then look for items that are different like a remodeled kitchen, pool, or oversized lot, and make adjustments.

DO NOT make the mistake of thinking that maintenance items can be consider as improvements that increase value. Things such as a new roof or new heating/cooling system are really *maintenance items.*

While these items may make your home sell faster, they typically DO NOT add much to the potential asking price of the home. After all, a buyer will **expect** a home to have a roof that does not leak and a properly functioning heating/cooling system!

As a pricing example, let's say that there are 4 homes similar to yours that have recently sold, priced at $166,500, $169,900, $179,000, and $183,900. The home at $183,900 has some extra features that your home does not have, but yours is superior to the one that sold for $166,500. Overall, the two other homes are pretty close to yours.

This gives you a current price range of $169,900 to $179,000. Now all you have to do is pick a price within this range!

Once you determine the proper price range for your home, how quickly you want to sell will dictate whether you price at the lower or higher ends of the price range. This is where your own time requirements come into play.

Your own personal situation will have some effect on the price you ask for your home. It is easy to see that if you needed to sell your home within 4 days, you would have to price it lower than if you had 4 months to sell it.

If you were not in a major rush, but still wanted a sale in a reasonable amount of time, you might decide on an asking price of $175,000.

If you are still having difficulty determining the proper price for your home, you can call us for assistance - no obligation, of course - or hire an appraiser which you can find listed in the phone book.

It is natural for every homeowner to have a certain "pride of ownership" and to think that their home should be worth more than the one down the street. This is where you must be objective, and try to take your emotional attachments to your home out of the situation.

You must be reasonable. **Unless you are in a total seller's market, if you price your home too high IT WILL NOT SELL!!!!!** It will sit on the market for months on end, getting the reputation of a "problem property".

People will assume that since the home has not sold, there must be something wrong with it. They will start to avoid it like the plague!

Even if you then drop the price, the damage is already done - the stigma is there, and you may need to drop the price even further to entice skeptical buyers.

DO NOT FALL INTO THIS TRAP!

Improper pricing is the single biggest mistake that sellers make. Don't let this happen to you. Make sure that you set a reasonable price for your home right from the start.

4. CALCULATING YOUR BOTTOM LINE

Step #2 - Calculating Your Bottom Line

Once you have determined a fair market price for your home, you can calculate your bottom line. This is the amount that you will net - get a check for - after paying all of the expenses associated with selling a home.

Remember, by selling your home yourself, the only costs which you avoid is the real estate agent's commission. You will still have to pay all of the other closing costs - just like any other seller.

Closing costs vary from area to area and also depend on how each individual contract is structured. The following are items that you may need to deduct from your sales price to determine your net proceeds:

> **MORTAGES OR LOANS** - Any first, second, etc. loans, or mortgages. Also any liens that occurred if you used your home as collateral. Call or write your lender and ask for the amount to pay the loan in full - often not the same as the principal balance).

> **LOAN DISCOUNT POINTS** - In many areas it is customary for the seller to pay points on the buyer's loan. This is negotiable, except on certain government loans. One point is equal to one percent of the loan amount - not the sales price.

For example, if the sales price was $175,000, and the buyer put a 10% down payment of $17,500, the loan amount would be $157,500. One discount point would be $1,575, two points would be $3,150, etc.

- **PRORATED INTEREST** - Mortgage interest is generally charged in arrears. This means that when you make your July payment, you are actually paying interest for June. So if your home sale closes on July 26th, you will still owe interest for 26 days even though you already made your payment on July 1st.

- **BUYER'S CLOSING COSTS** - Many buyers will ask the seller to pay part or all of their closing costs. On some government loans it is required by law that the seller pays them. These costs can include, but are not limited to: loan application fees, credit Book, loan origination fee (usually 1% of the loan amount), loan discount points, title, escrow, and attorney's fees, funding fees, tax service, mortgage insurance premiums, and impounds for taxes, insurance, and interest.

- **ATTORNEY FEES** - Everyone loves lawyers! Attorneys draw up the closing documents, but they do not represent the buyer, or the seller, or the title company.

- **ESCROW FEES** - Escrow companies are disinterested third parties that hold funds, handle paperwork, and make sure that all necessary conditions are met before releasing money or transferring title.

- **TRANSFER TAXES I CHARGES** - Transfer fees are often charged by state or local governments as a way to increase revenue. They vary widely, and are often based on a percentage of the sales price.

- **APPRAISAL FEES** - If the buyer is obtaining new financing for the purchase, the lender will require a professional appraisal on the house. This is another negotiable item, but is often paid by the buyer in this area.

- **TERMITE INSPECTIONS** - Required on some government loans, and requested by many buyers. The inspection fee should really be paid by the buyer because the buyer should want all inspectors to work on their behalf rather than the seller's. But this is a negotiable expense item.

- **STRUCTURAL I GENERAL INSPECTIONS** - Professional independent inspection services are required by law in some areas and often requested by buyers to make them more confident about the purchase. Again, this fee should really be paid by the buyer because the buyer should want all inspectors to work on their behalf rather than the seller's. But this is a negotiable expense item.

- **TITLE INSURANCE FEES** - Title insurance protects the buyer and lender against issues of improper ownership or transfer. The title insurance company will research the title to make sure there are no liens, judgments, or clouds on the title that would affect the ownership rights.

- **HOMEOWNER ASSOCIATION FEES** - If the area has an HOA (Homeowners' Association), chances are that there will be a fee to transfer the account from one owner to the next.

- **PREPAYMENT PENALTIES** - Many private and some conventional loans have specific monetary penalties if the loan is paid off prior to a certain date. Typically, loans made by Texas lenders have no prepayment penalties.

- **RECONVEYANCE FEES** - This fee may be charged by an attorney or escrow company to clear off the lien on the title when your existing loan is paid off at closing.

- **FAILURE TO NOTIFY PENALTIES** - Some government lenders can charge one extra month's interest if you fail to notify them at least 30 days in advance of your intent to pay off the loan.

- **ASSUMPTION FEES** - Loans that are being assumed by the buyer often have an assumption fee charged by the lender.

- **HOME WARRANTY COVERAGE** - Depending on the plan, a home warranty covers items in the house - air conditioning/heating system, hot water heater, built-in appliances, etc. - for a period of usually one year.

For a list of specific charges, you can contact a title/escrow office, mortgage lender, or a real estate attorney. Of course, we would be happy to provide you with a thorough net proceeds analysis at ***no cost or obligation***.

After completing the first two steps in the process, it is entirely possible that may decide not to sell after all. Perhaps the market values are not what you had thought, and you will not be able to net enough money on the sale to be able to accomplish your next goal.

The important thing is to accept the realities of the market. ***If the timing is not right for you, it isn't right!***

5. PREPARING YOUR HOME FOR SALE

Step #3 - Preparing Your Home For Sale

Properly preparing your home for sale can make the difference between a quick sale at full price, and a home that sits unsold for months - even after several price reductions.

The first order of business is to forget your emotional attachment to your home and look at it through the eyes of a potential buyer. Be impartial, and recognize the weaknesses of your home.

How does it stack up?

Remember, potential buyers are going to be viewing lots of other homes, and if yours does not stand out, it will be much more difficult to sell.

Buyers buy what they see. **If what they see is dirty, messy, and worn looking, you do not stand a chance!**

It is just like if you were going to sell your car. The first thing you would do is clean and "detail" the car inside and out. Your house is no different!!

With a mental picture of a model home in your mind, make an "attack list" of items to be completed on your home. It may be a short or a long list, depending on the condition of your home, but keep in mind that all your efforts now will pay off big on closing day.

The objective is to make your home appear well maintained, spacious, organized, and clean. Many factors such as how light it is, the colors, sounds and smell subtly affect the buyer's impression of your home.

Start by walking out to the middle of the street and take a good, focused look at the overall appearance of the exterior of your home. Good "curb appeal" will make the critical proper first impression. ***Remember, if a home is unattractive from the outside, buyer will not bother to see the inside!!***

This means well-groomed, healthy looking lawn, trees, shrubs, and flower beds. Check your driveway and clean any oil stains with cleaning solutions, and move any old vehicles, trailers, or boats off the premises to a storage facility. Replace or repair any loose or missing roof shingles or tiles. If needed, replace or repaint the mailbox.

Your front door is a focal point of potential buyers. Make sure it is scrubbed clean or completely refinished if necessary. Fix any broken windows or screens. Completely repainting the exterior of your home may be necessary if it is peeling or blistering, but often simply doing the trim, window sashes, shutters, and garage door is sufficient.

Remove any political or other signs. Now do the same to the side and rear yards.

Remove all debris, junk, and clutter. Clean and neatly arrange any lawn furniture, barbecues, etc.

Next, move to the inside of your home. Begin with a complete, top to bottom, military-style scrubbing of every room, nook, and cranny.   Be especially diligent in the kitchen and bathrooms, which should pass the white glove test. **CLEAN HOUSES SELL!**

Attack the garage and other storage areas, if you have them. Now is the time to get rid of any old junk, and clean and organize everything else.

If the interior has not been painted in several years, you should probably go ahead and do it.   A fresh coat of white or off-white paint will make the place look bigger and lighter, and give it a "new" smell.   It does not cost that much, and makes a big difference in buyer perception.   If not, do a thorough job of touch-up painting.

Have the carpet cleaned. If it is worn, replace it. This is a fairly big cost, but it makes a huge difference in how the home shows. You should more than make up for the expense with a faster sale at a higher price.

Install the highest intensity bulbs allowable in all the light fixtures. This will make the rooms appear larger, brighter, and more cheerful. Clean all windows and curtains/blinds.

Clean out the closets to make them look bigger. Store out of season clothes elsewhere and neatly arrange what is left. Too much clutter will make a home feel small and disorganized.   Move out excess furniture, especially worn or outdated items, and take down pictures that hide the walls.   Clean off the magnets from the refrigerator, and box up any other clutter-causing nick-knacks.

Clean all the heating/cooling system vents, and replace the filters. Fix or replace all of the little things that you have been meaning to get to. Make sure that **everything** is working properly - toilets, appliances, doorbell, etc.

If you have lived in your home for a while, by the time you finish with your attack list you will probably have truckloads of stuff to sell, give away to charity, or take to the dump. **Your motto should be: "If in doubt, move it out!"**

Consider having a huge garage sale. Not only will you reduce the clutter in your home, but you can use the proceeds to pay for some of your touch-ups and repairs. Plus, movers charge by the pound, so you will save there, too!

Make sure that your cars are clean as well. It all adds to the impression that you are people that take good care of your things.

If you smoke, DO NOT SMOKE IN THE HOUSE!! A smoky-smelling house turns buyers off faster than nuclear waste - *even buyers who smoke themselves!* If you have smoked in the house much, you will probably need to paint the interior, and have the carpets, drapes, and furniture professionally cleaned.

This brings us to pets. While household pets may be nice for everyday living, they are one of your worst enemies when it is time to sell. If you have pets, you will have pet odors, whether you notice them or not. About 25% of prospective buyers will not consider a home with pets in it - either because they have allergies, or simply think it is dirty. Plus, a dog barking, sniffing, and scratching hardly makes a potential buyer feel relaxed and comfortable.

If at all possible, see if a neighbor, friend, or relative will take the animal until the home is sold. I know you may be quite attached to your pet and this may be a touchy subject, but it is up to you if you want a sale for top dollar.

It can be a lot of work, but it will be worth it. Clean, organized, clutter-free homes are always the first to sell!!!

6. <u>MARKETING AND SHOWING YOUR HOME</u>

Step #4 - Marketing and Showing Your Home

Now that your home is ready, it is time to find some interested buyers to show it to. The effort required to attract potential purchasers depends on the current market conditions in your area.

If you are in the midst of a seller's market where there is a shortage of homes for sale, simply throwing a FOR SALE sign out in the yard can produce a frenzy of activity.

Unfortunately, most markets are nowhere near that good for sellers, so you better plan on putting in some long hours. You are competing with all of the other homes for sale, and the competition is often fierce.

The first step in your marketing plan is to put up a FOR SALE sign in the front yard. Before you run down to the corner drug store, keep in mind that a cheap, flimsy look sign does not convey the quality image that you want. Invest some money in a nice looking, quality sign that will last longer than the first rain storm.

It should be at least as nice as the ones that the real estate agents use. Call some sign painters and get some bids.

Next, put together a professional looking brochure that communicates all of the features and benefits of your home. Include a nice picture of your home and touch on such items as proximity to schools, shopping, major transportation routes, major employers, and recreation areas.

Also cover neighborhood amenities, age, appearance, condition, bedrooms, bathrooms, type and style, landscaping, garage, kitchen, family room, laundry, pool/spa, etc.

Do not forget financial information such as the price, down payment, monthly payment, year round utility expenses, property taxes, what items are included in the sale - such as appliances, shelving, etc. - and, of course, directions to the house, along with your name, address, and phone number.

A representative from a local mortgage company should be willing to provide you will all of the information you will need regarding loan programs, down payments, interests rates, monthly payments, etc.

With personal computers, desktop publishing is much easier than ever before. If you have access to a computer, you should be able to put together a nice looking brochure if you take your time and think it through.   Please - **_no junky looking flyers!_**

If you cannot do it yourself, sketch out a rough draft by hand and take it along with a picture of your home to a quick-print shop. They should be able to fix you up fairly inexpensively.

Once you have your brochures, you need to have a weatherproof information box to put them in next to - or attached to - the yard sign. The box should read: **FREE INFO-PLEASE TAKE ONE.** Monitor the box and keep it full.

Also pass out the brochures to all of your friends and neighbors, pass them out at area businesses, drop some off at the relocation office of any large employers in the area, and put them up on bulletin boards wherever possible.

Now write a good, enthusiastic sounding ad to run in the newspaper. Try to make your ad stand out from the others. It is important to have an attention-getting HEADLINE such as:

"MOVING TO FLORIDA"

"DIVORCE FORCES SALE"

"MUST SELL QUICKLY"

"WALK TO SCHOOL"

"OUR LOSS, YOUR GAIN"

"YOU WILL NOT BELIEVE THIS"

"SPACIOUS HOME NEEDS LOVING FAMILY"

"ENJOY PRIVACY"

Test different ads and see what the responses are. You can try running a different ad each week, or a different one in separate publications.

Focus on the benefits of your home. Do not write a boring ad that sounds like all the others and will get lost in the crowd. Stress items such as views, Quiet Street, landscaping, master bedroom, kitchen, and family room.

The whole purpose of the ad is to get your phone to ring!!!

THIS MEANS THAT SOMEONE NEEDS TO ANSWER IT, WHEN IT DOES RING!!!!!

The biggest complaint that buyers have with For Sale by Owners is that **no one answers the phone** when they call - or they get a child or babysitter that is not prepared to handle the call properly.

You are competing against professionals. You need to be home, or utilize a cellular phone, call forwarding, or pager. If a buyer cannot get through to you, they often just go on to the next ad or call a real estate agent.

Keep a copy of your brochure next to the phone, it can help you stay organized and not miss any features when callers inquire. If callers do not want to set an appointment yet, offer to mail them a brochure.

Also keep a call log handy, so you will know how many calls you are getting from which ads, and to keep track of names and phone numbers.

Look into all possible avenues to market your home - web sites, door hangers, neighborhood newsletters, etc.

An Open House can help get your home exposed to the market. Get some directional Open House signs and place them at corners leading to your home from major streets, and one in front of your house. Make sure to check local regulations before placing signs. You also may want to run an advertisement in the newspaper.

We are now going to suggest an option that can add a large amount of exposure to your home and still save your half of the normal commission you would pay an agent. Before you have a heart attack, we are NOT talking about listing it with an agent. You do not have to use this option, but in most markets, it makes a lot of sense.

On your sign and in all of your ads, insert the words: "AGENTS WELCOME". When agents call, tell them that you **are not listing with an agent,** but that you will be happy to pay them a 3% commission if they bring you a buyer that successfully buys your home.

This commission is about the same as an agent would make if they sold another agent's listing, and a majority of homes are sold by an agent other than the listing agent.

This option can generate a lot of additional interest in your home. If an agent does end up selling it, not only will you still save a substantial amount compared to a full commission, but you will have professional assistance along the way, as well.

Once you have attracted interested buyers, it is time to show your home. This is where all your time and effort in preparing your home will really pay off!!!

Before you set an appointment, make sure that the buyer is looking for what you have. If they need 6 bedrooms and you only have three, they probably will not be serious about your home.

Also take a few minutes to politely "qualify" the buyer by asking questions about how long they have been on the job, do they own a home currently, have they been pre-approved for a loan by a lender, etc.

DO NOT waste your time showing your home to prospects who cannot afford to buy it!!!!!

Also, a few words of caution. People are not always who they seem, and you can never be too careful. One look at the newspaper or evening news is proof enough.

It is recommended that you note the license number of their car and ask for identification prior to letting strangers into your home. Serious buyers will not mind, especially when you cheerfully tell them that it is simply a security precaution that was recommended to you by a professional.

Stash all small valuables out of sight. Even though you will try to stay with the prospects as they tour your home, you never can watch them completely.

It is probably a wise idea for women to avoid showing the home without someone else present. This is not intended to be sexist, just cautious. You decide for yourself.

Okay, it is SHOW TIME!!!

To get the most out of every showing, there are certain procedures you should follow, both prior to the prospects arrival and after they come inside.

Shortly before the appointment, open all of the drapes and blinds and turn on all the lights - even in the daytime. Turn off the TV and put some soft music on at a low volume. Set the thermostats so that it is not too hot or cold. If you have children, send them to a friend's house, or put them on their best behavior.

If you still have pets in the house, get them out and freshen the air. Make sure all of the beds are made and do a quick pick-up throughout.

When the buyers arrive, your home should sell itself. Be friendly and cheerful, and try to make them feel comfortable. Hand them your brochure, and take them on a tour of the property.

Show the most appealing parts of your home first. Casually point out all of the features and benefits of your home, but do not oversell or say stupid things like "this is the kitchen".

If they are not interested, they will probably politely thank you and head for the front door!   Do not take it personally, the layout or something else about the house probably just does not fit their personal needs.

If the buyers are interested, you will know it. They will stay longer, and ask lots of questions.

If they show serious interest, do not be afraid to suggest that they buy it!

It is time to get a signed contract!

7. <u>NEGOTIATION AND CONTRACT</u>

Step #5 - Negotiation and Contract

Being familiar with the market conditions and knowing your personal motivation to sell will guide you in the negotiations.

Get a standard real estate purchase contract and make sure that you are completely familiar with it and how to fill it out. Review it with a real estate attorney if you are not comfortable.

Generally, the buyer will present you with an offer for you to consider. In Texas, only written contracts for the purchase of real estate are enforceable, so make sure it is in writing, not merely verbal.

The buyer may not have the proper forms, so always make sure to have several contracts ready to go.

Starting negotiations face to face with the buyer with both of you staring at a blank page can be a bit awkward, but just keep your objectives in mind and forge ahead. Politely but firmly take control of the situation.

This is where things can get a little sticky, and you will need to have done your homework. Having a contract that is not worded properly can put you into a real hornet's nest!

Make sure to spell out every little detail in the contract. A misunderstanding - honest or otherwise - could end up costing you thousands of dollars or even tying your home up for months.

When you are presented with an offer from a buyer, you have four basic options:

1. **Accept the offer as presented**

2. **Reject the offer as presented**

3. **Make a counter offer**

4. **Do nothing**

Here are some items that you should consider when structuring an offer or deciding how to respond to an offer that is presented to you:

1. **Price**

2. **Down Payment**

3. **Earnest Money Deposit**

4. **Is the Buyer Pre-Approved?**

5. **Is the Interest Rate They Want Available?**

6. **Closing and Possession Dates**

7. **Proration's**

8. **Loan Discount Points-Who Pays Them?**

9. **Closing Costs-Who Pays What?**

10. **Appraisal-Who Pays?**

11. **Home Protection Plan-Who Pays and How Much?**

12. Inspections-What Type and Who Pays?

13. Items Included-Washer, Dryer, Refrigerator, Etc.

14. Title Company and/or Attorney

15. Contingencies-What and How Long?

16. Option Period-Yes Or No; If Yes, At What Price and How Long?

Contingencies may seem like a minor issue, but they can be a major stumbling block. A contingency means that something else must happen in order for the deal to go through.

A purchase may be contingent on the buyer getting approved for financing, selling the home that they already own, getting a favorable inspection Book, or any number of other things.

Make the contingencies as specific as possible, and spell out exactly what will happen if the contingency is or is not met. Also try to make them self-canceling. For example: *"If a buyer does not object in writing within 14 days from acceptance of this offer, contingency shall be considered removed."*

Spending some extra time to make sure that the contract is "clean" can save you enormous headaches down the road!

Once you have a contract mutually agreed upon and signed by all parties, take it with the buyer's earnest money deposit to an escrow company or real estate attorney.

8. CLOSING AND MOVING

Step #6 - Closing and Moving

You are on the home stretch, almost there!!! Now is not the time to get lazy or drop the ball.

Once all of the terms and conditions of the contract are agreed upon by you and the buyer, you will really need to stay on top of things on a daily basis. There are at least a hundred things that can go wrong and foul up the sale.

You will probably be dealing with a mortgage company, title company, escrow company or attorney, appraiser, and inspector, among others. Make certain that the buyer's deposit check clears the bank, that their credit Book and other financial information is okay, and that all deadlines and contingencies are met.

Make darn sure that everything is in order BEFORE you start loading things into the moving truck. You do not want to have to put the house back on the market after you have moved out! Plus, once you move out, the buyer has a lot more leverage to get you to alter the contract in their favor.

Do not forget the little details like transferring the utilities out of your name, and change of address for U.S. mail and newspapers.

There you have it. If you have taken the time and energy to handle your sale properly, you will be rewarded with a nice proceeds check from the escrow company or attorney's office!

We hope that you have found this Book to be a valuable source of information to aid you in selling your home yourself. If you follow the tips and recommendations outlined here, you will be way ahead of most others attempting to sell their homes.

Every home sale is unique, so if you have any questions that we can help you with, please do not hesitate to call us. As we mentioned before - **We are not like most other agents!**

Any time you call us, you can count on knowledgeable assistance **without** any obligation, pressure, gimmicks, or sales pitches.

Kirk Austin can be reached at 512-574-0667

www.KirkAustinSellsHomes.com

www.KirkAustinBuysHouses.com

ABOUT THE AUTHOR

Kirk Austin is a licensed Real Estate professional. He is devoted to helping people own a piece of America. Kirk can help you sell or buy a property and is available to answers question, at any time. Visit; KirkAustinSellsHomes.com and KirkAustinBuysHouses.com